The GOSPELS BOOK *of* DAYS

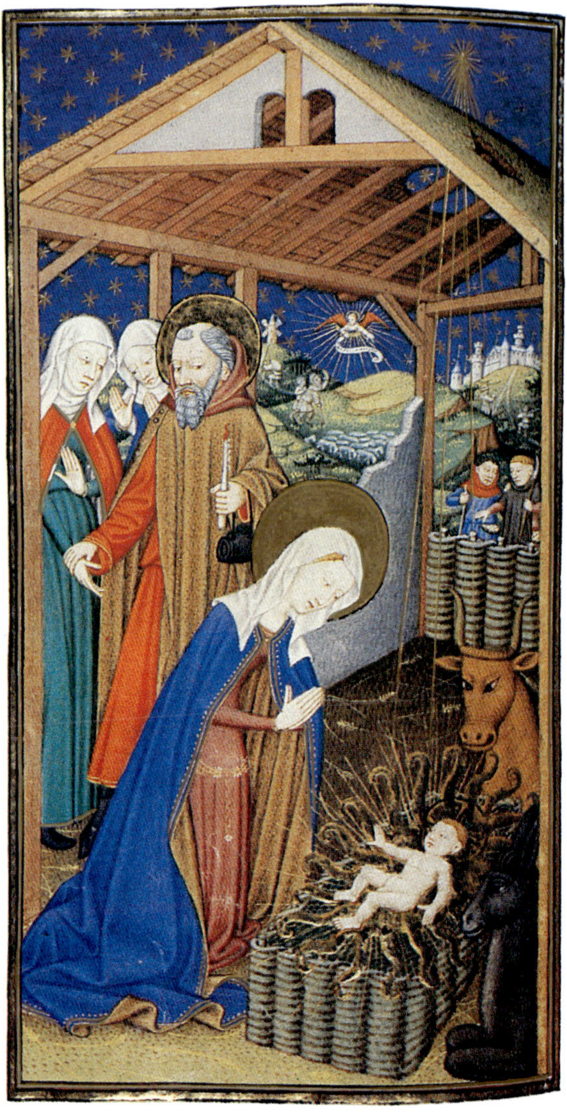

The GOSPELS BOOK *of* DAYS

ACCORDING TO ST. MATTHEW ST. MARK ST. LUKE & ST. JOHN

EBURY PRESS STATIONERY

Published in 1993 by Ebury Press Stationery
An imprint of Random House UK Ltd
Random House, 20 Vauxhall Bridge Road,
London SW1V 2SA

Copyright © Random House UK Ltd 1993

All rights reserved. No part of this book may be reproduced
in any form or by any means without permission in writing
from the publisher.

ISBN 0 09 177481 0

Set in Goudy Old Style

by SX Composing, Rayleigh, Essex

Printed in Singapore

Designed by David Fordham

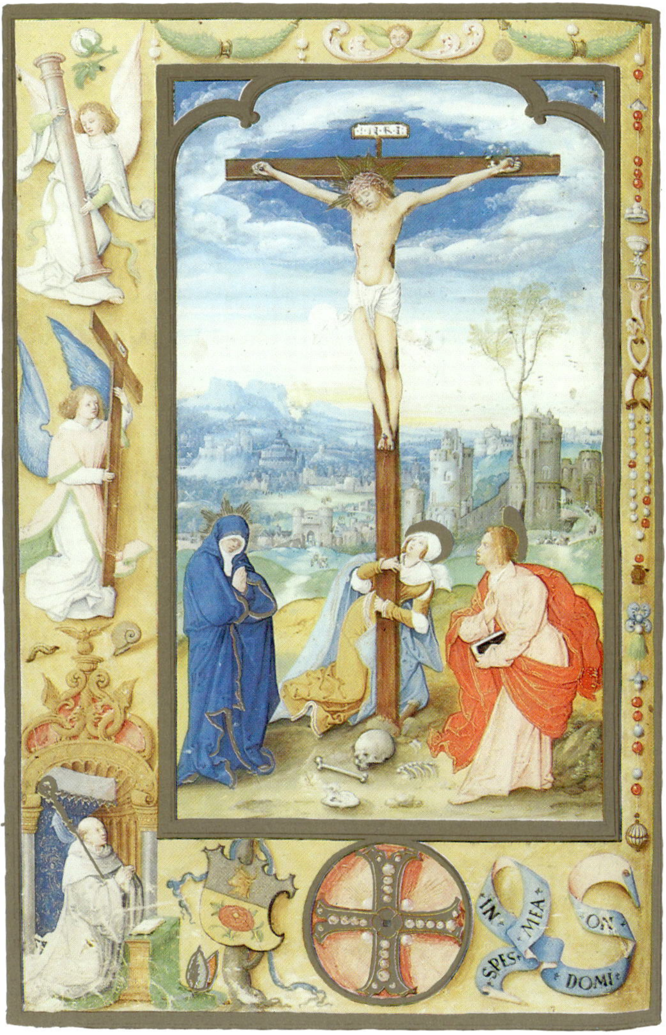
IN
MEA
ON
SPES
DOMI

1

2

3

4

5

6

7

JANUARY

And the Angel said unto them, Fear not: for, behold, I bring you good tidings of great joy, which shall be to all people.

ST LUKE 2:10

8

9

10

11

12

13

14

JANUARY

And when they were come into the house, they saw the young child
with Mary his mother, and fell down, and worshipped him: and
when they had opened their treasures, they presented unto him gifts;
gold, and frankincense, and myrrh.

ST MATTHEW 2:11

15

16

17

18

19

20

21

JANUARY

Behold, the angel of the Lord appeareth to Joseph in a dream, saying, Arise, and take the young child and his mother, and flee into Egypt, and be thou there until I bring thee word: for Herod will seek the young child to destroy him.
When he arose, he took the young child and his mother by night, and departed into Egypt.
ST MATTHEW 2:13-14

22

23

24

25

26

27

28

JANUARY

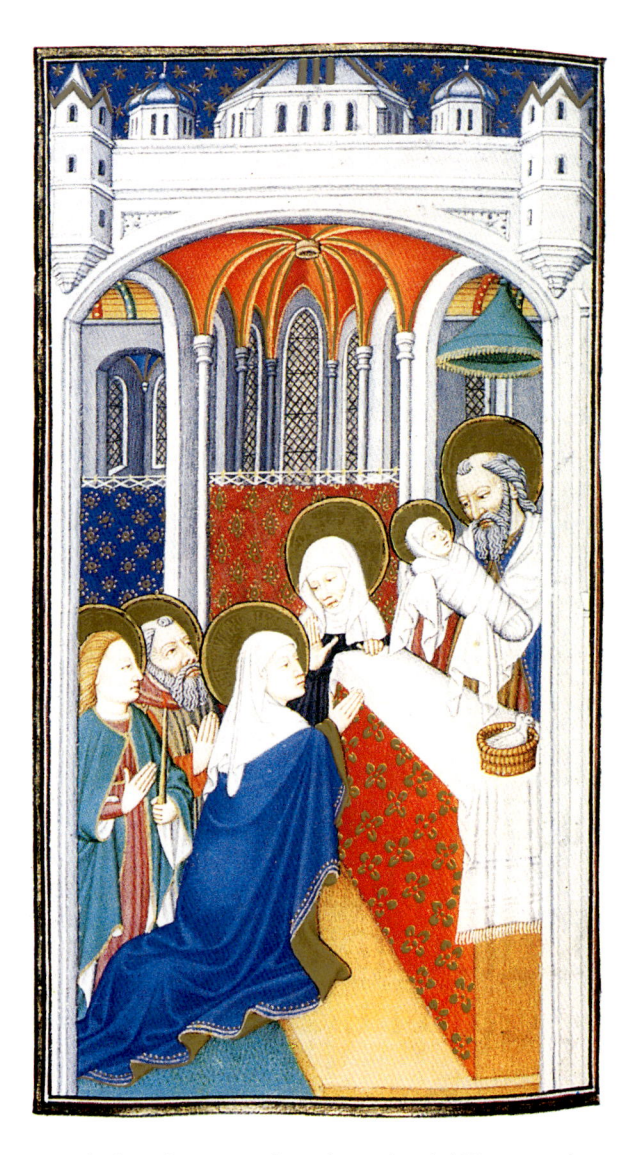

And when the parents brought in the child Jesus, to do
for him after the custom of the law, Then took he him
up in his arms, and blessed God.

ST LUKE 2:27-28

29	
30	
31	
1	
2	
3	
4	

JAN – FEB

And Jesus, when he was baptized, went up straightway out of the water: and, lo, the heavens were opened unto him, and he saw the Spirit of God descending like a dove, and lighting upon him.

ST MATTHEW 3:16

5

6

7

8

9

10

11

FEBRUARY

The next day John seeth Jesus coming unto him, and saith, Behold
the Lamb of God, which taketh away the sin of the world.

ST JOHN 1:29

12

13

14

15

16

17

18

FEBRUARY

And as they did eat, Jesus took bread, and blessed, and brake it, and gave to them, and said, Take, eat: this is my body.

ST MARK 14:22

19

20

21

22

23

24

25

✣ FEBRUARY ✣

For this is my blood of the new testament, which is
shed for many for the remission of sins.
ST MATTHEW 26:28

26

27

28

29

1

2

3

✣ FEB – MARCH ✣

After that he poureth water into a bason, and began to
wash the disciples' feet, and to wipe them with the
towel wherewith he was girded.

ST JOHN 13:5

4

5

6

7

8

9

10

✜ MARCH ✜

And being in an agony he prayed more earnestly: and his sweat was
as it were great drops of blood falling down to the ground.
ST LUKE 22:44

11

12

13

14

15

16

17

MARCH

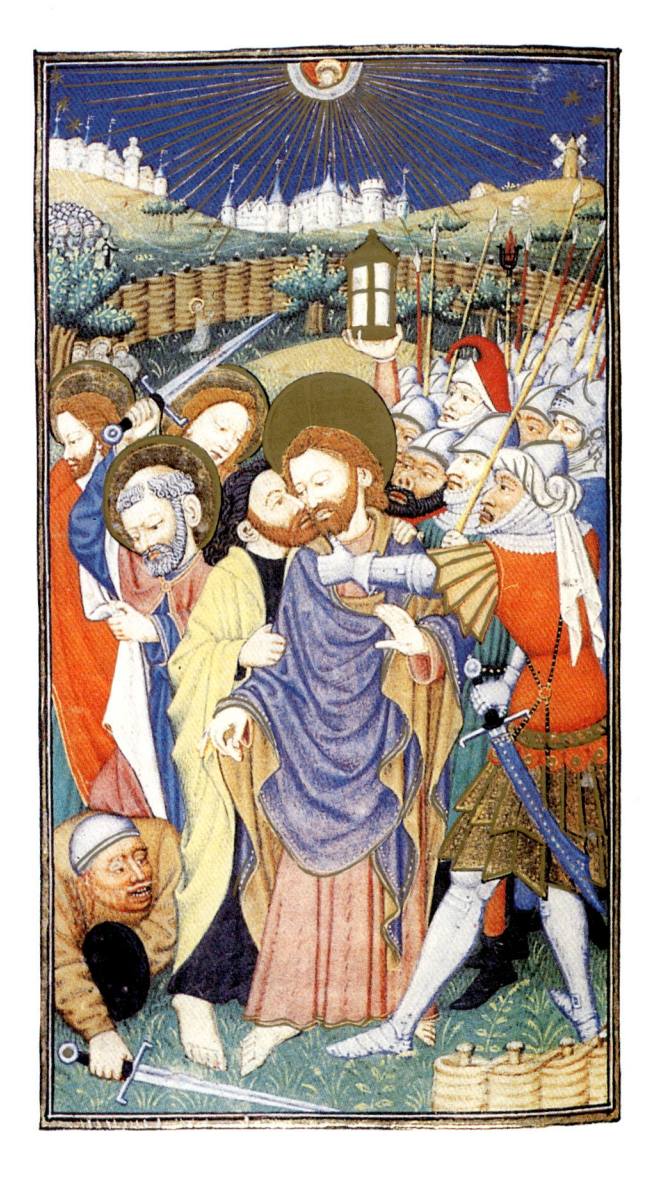

But Jesus said unto him, Judas, betrayest thou the Son
of man with a kiss?

ST LUKE 22:48

18

19

20

21

22

23

24

MARCH

Then the band and the captain and officers of the Jews
took Jesus, and bound him.
ST JOHN 18:12

25

26

27

28

29

30

31

MARCH

And the whole multitude of them arose, and led him
unto Pilate. And they began to accuse him.

ST LUKE 23:1-2

1

2

3

4

5

6

7

APRIL

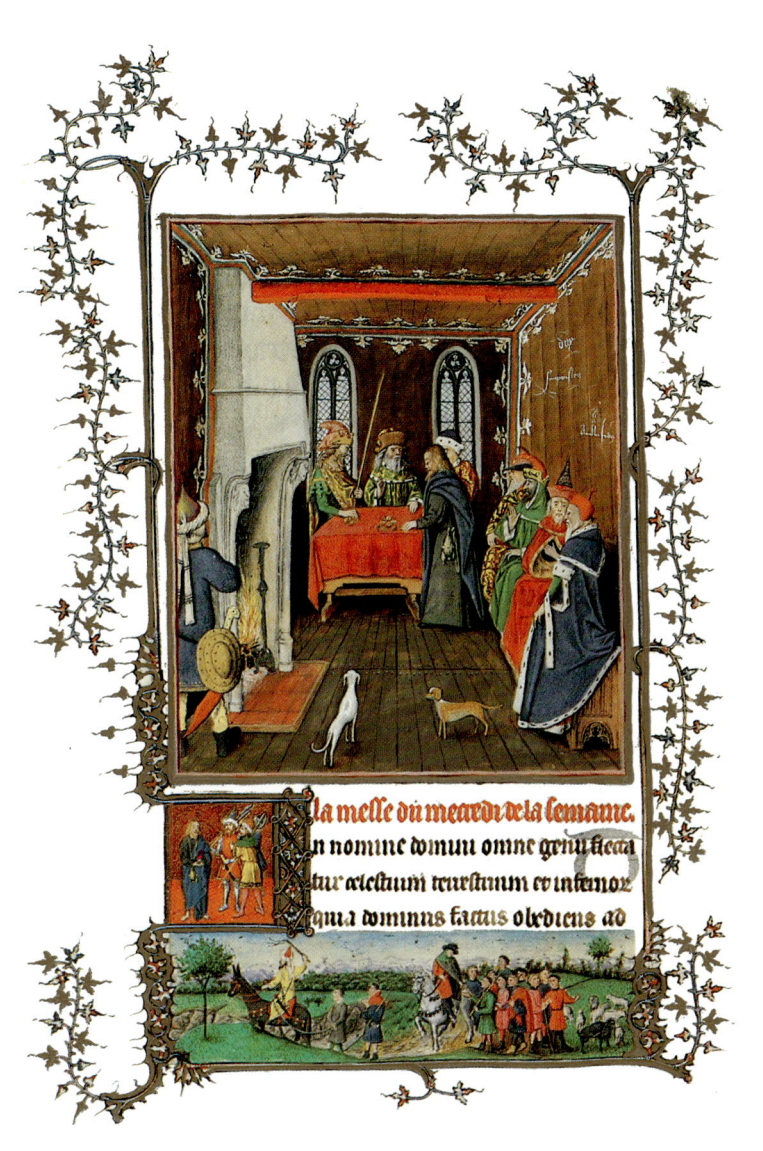

la messe du mcaredi de la semaine.
n nomine domini omne genu flecta
tur celestium terrestrium et infernor
quia dominus factus obediens ad

Then Judas, which had betrayed him, when he saw that he was
condemned, repented himself, and brought again the thirty pieces of
silver to the chief priests and elders.

ST MATTHEW 27:3

8

9

10

11

12

13

14

APRIL

And they smote him on the head with a reed, and did spit upon him, and bowing their knees worshipped him.

ST MARK 15:19

15

16

17

18

19

20

21

APRIL

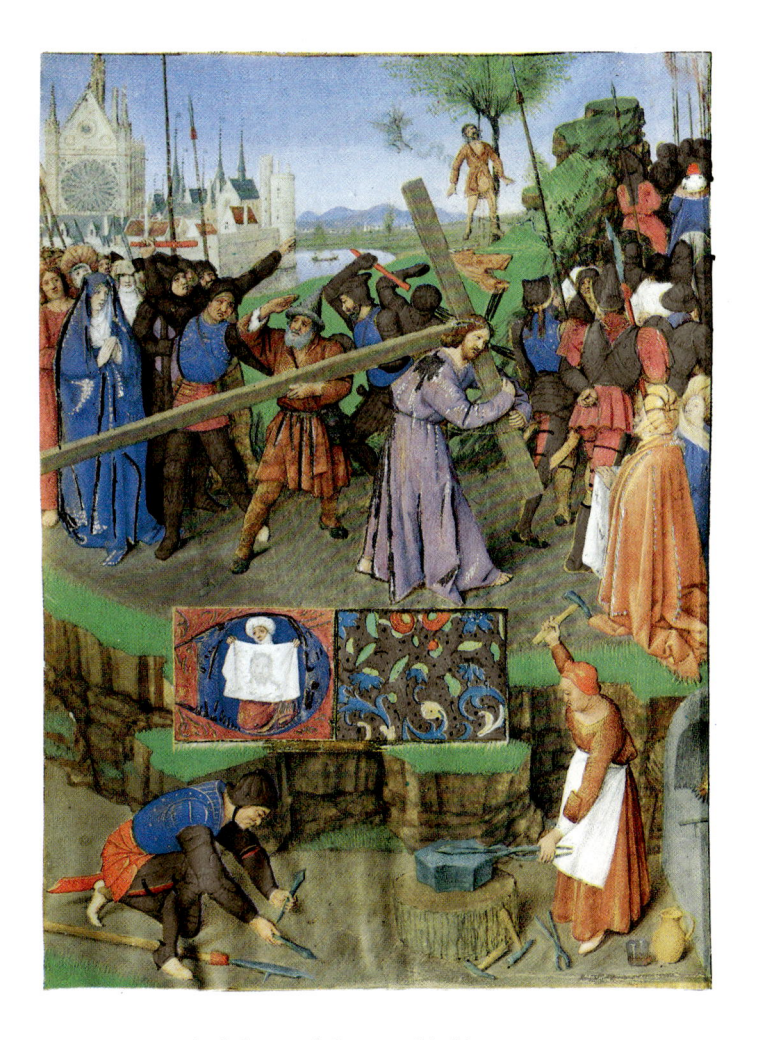

And they took Jesus and led him away.
And he bearing his cross went forth into a place called
the place of a skull, which is called in the Hebrew
Golgotha.

ST JOHN 19:16-17

22

23

24

25

26

27

28

APRIL

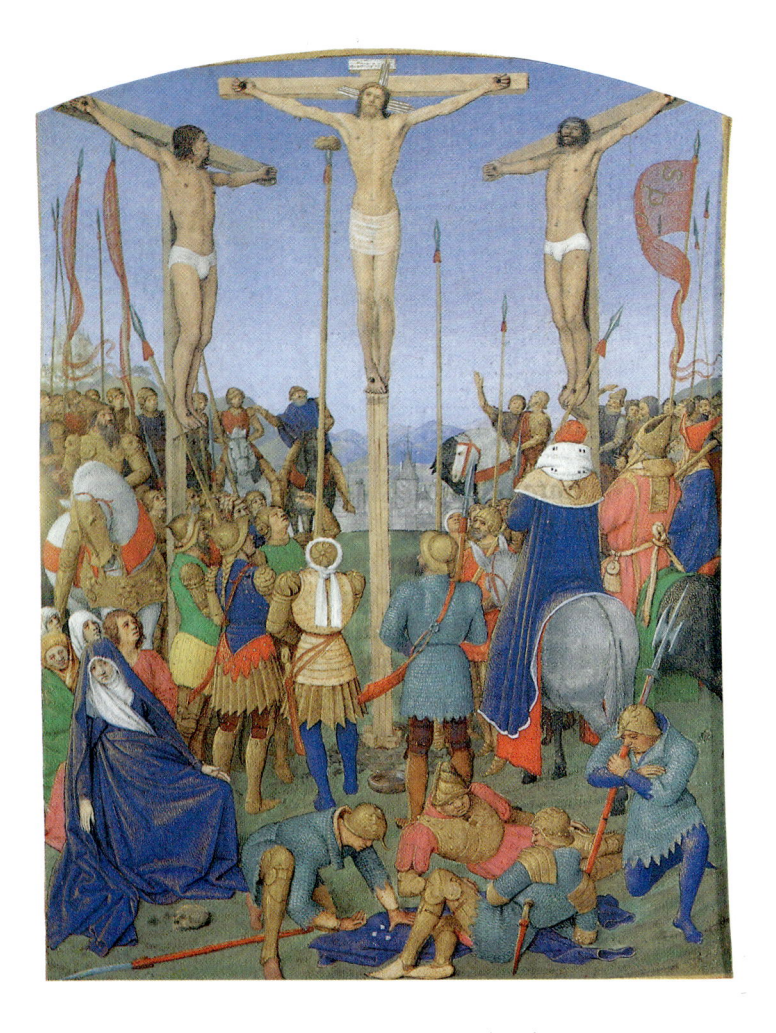

And straightway one of them ran, and took a spunge,
and filled it with vinegar, and put it on a reed, and
gave him to drink.

ST MATTHEW 27:48

29

30

1

2

3

4

5

APRIL – MAY

But one of the soldiers with a spear pierced his side,
and forthwith came there out blood and water.

ST JOHN 19:34

6

7

8

9

10

11

12

MAY

There were also women looking on afar off: among whom was Mary Magdalene, and Mary the mother of James the less and of Joses, and Salome.

ST MARK 15:40

13

14

15

16

17

18

19

MAY

This man went unto Pilate, and begged the body of Jesus. And he took it down, and wrapped it in linen.

ST LUKE 23:52-53

20

21

22

23

24

25

26

MAY

The Son of man must be delivered into the hands of sinful men, and
be crucified, and the third day rise again.

ST LUKE 24:7

27

| 28 |

| 29 |

| 30 |

| 31 |

| 1 |

| 2 |

MAY – JUNE

After that he appeared in another form unto two of them, as they walked, and went into the country.
ST MARK 16:12

3

4

5

6

7

8

9

JUNE

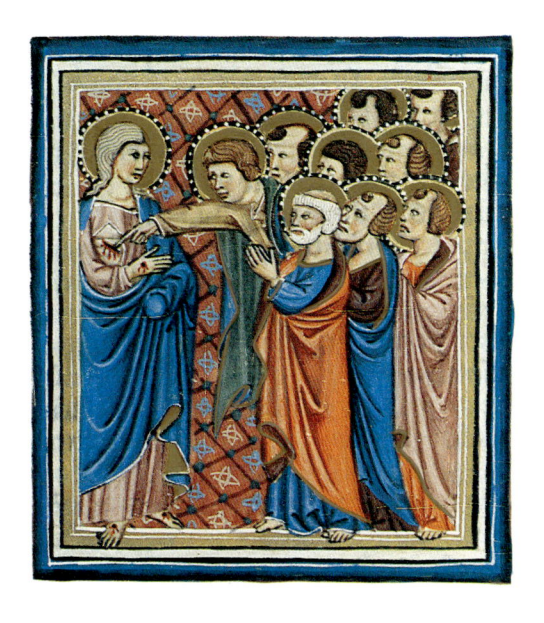

Then saith he to Thomas, Reach hither thy
finger, and behold my hands; and reach hither
thy hand, and thrust it into my side: and be not
faithless, but believing.

ST JOHN 20:27

10

11

12

13

14

15

16

JUNE

And they went forth, and preached every where, the Lord working
with them, and confirming the word with signs following.

ST MARK 16:20

17

18

19

20

21

22

23

JUNE

And he led them out as far as to Bethany, and he lifted up his hands,
and blessed them.

ST LUKE 24:50

24

25

26

27

28

29

30

JUNE

And it came to pass, while he blessed them, he was
parted from them, and carried up into heaven.
ST LUKE 24:51

1

2

3

4

5

6

7

JULY

So then after the Lord had spoken unto them, he was received up into heaven, and sat on the right hand of God.

ST MARK 16:19

8

9

10

11

12

13

14

✣ JULY ✣

And they worshipped him, and returned to Jerusalem
with great joy: And were continually in the temple,
praising and blessing God. Amen.

ST LUKE 24:52-53

15

16

17

18

19

20

21

JULY

ST. JOHN THE EVANGELIST

22

23

24

25

26

27

28

JULY

ST. LUKE

29

30

31

1

2

3

4

✣ JULY – AUGUST ✣

And Jesus being full of the Holy Ghost returned from
Jordan, and was led by the Spirit into the wilderness,
being forty days tempted of the devil. And in those
days he did eat nothing: and when they were ended, he
afterward hungered.

And the devil said unto him, If thou be the Son of
God, command this stone that it be made bread.
And Jesus answered him, saying, It is written, That
man shall not live by bread alone, but by every word of
God.

ST LUKE 4:1-4

5

6

7

8

9

10

11

AUGUST

Again, the devil taketh him up into an exceeding high mountain, and sheweth him all the kingdoms of the world, and the glory of them.

ST MATTHEW 4:8

12

13

14

15

16

17

18

AUGUST

John did baptize in the wilderness, and preach the
baptism of repentance for the remission of sins.
ST MARK 1:4

19

20

21

22

23

24

25

AUGUST

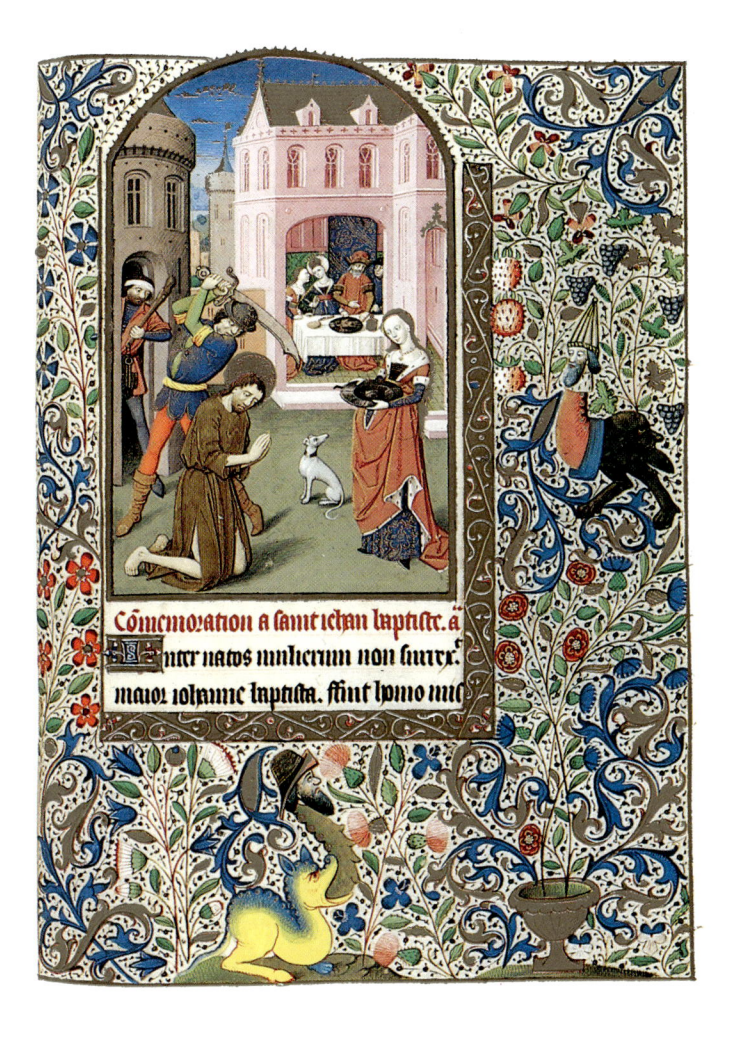

And immediately the king sent an executioner, and
commanded his head to be brought: and he went and
beheaded him in the prison.

ST MARK 6:27

26

27

28

29

30

31

1

AUG – SEPT

When the ruler of the feast had tasted the water that was made wine, and knew not whence it was: (but the servants which drew the water knew;) the governor of the feast called the bridegroom,
And saith unto him, Every man at the beginning doth set forth good wine; and when men have well drunk, then that which is worse: but thou has kept the good wine until now.

ST JOHN 2:9-10

2

3

4

5

6

7

8

✣ SEPTEMBER ✣

He went up into a mountain: And when he was set, his
disciples came unto him: And he opened his mouth,
and taught them.

ST MATTHEW 5:1-2

9

10

11

12

13

14

15

SEPTEMBER

And he healed many that were sick of divers diseases, and cast out many devils.

ST MARK 1:34

16

17

18

19

20

21

22

SEPTEMBER

And when the woman saw that she was not hid, she
came trembling, and falling down before him, she
declared unto him before all the people for what cause
she had touched him, and how she was healed
immediately.

ST LUKE 8:47

23

24

25

26

27

28

29

SEPTEMBER

When he had thus spoken, he spat on the ground, and
made clay of the spittle, and he anointed the eyes of
the blind man with the clay, And said unto him, Go,
wash in the pool of Siloam. He went his way therefore,
and washed, and came seeing.

ST JOHN 9:6-7

30
1
2
3
4
5
6

SEPT – OCT

And they did eat, and were all filled: and there was taken up of fragments that remained to them twelve baskets.

ST LUKE 9:17

7

8

9

10

11

12

13

✤ OCTOBER ✤

ILEXI qm exaudiet dominus: uoce orationis mee
qua inclinauit aurem suam michi: et in diebz meis inuocabo
Circumdederunt me dolores mor

And in hell he lifted up his eyes, being in torments, and seeth
Abraham afar off, and Lazarus in his bosom.

ST LUKE 16:23

14

15

16

17

18

19

20

OCTOBER

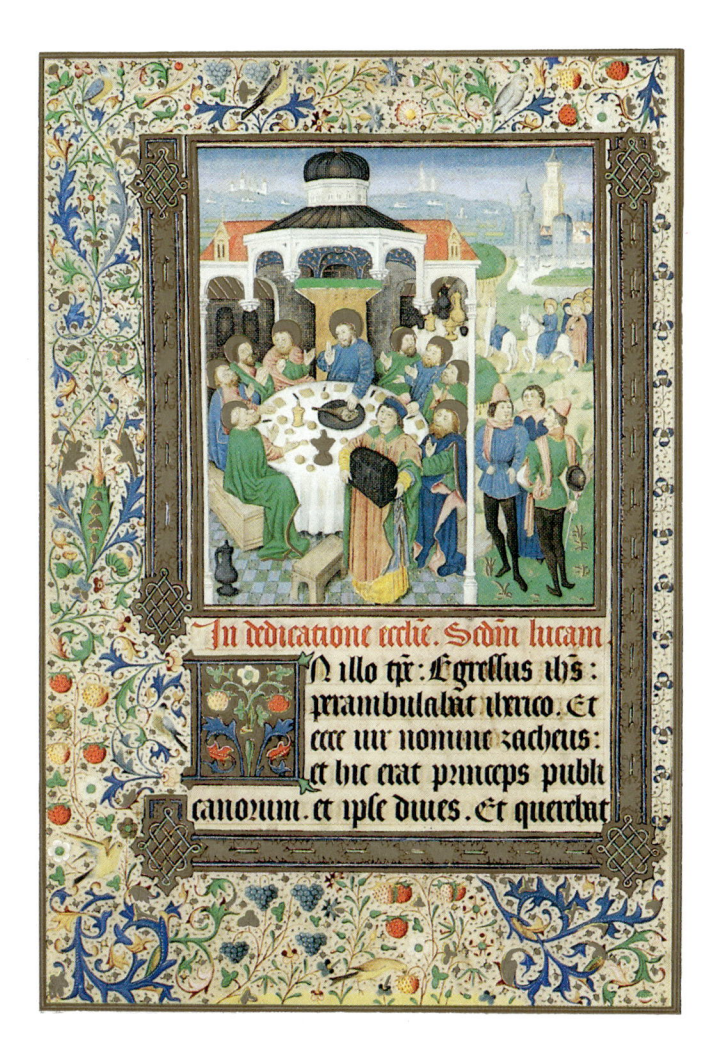

And Zacchaeus stood, and said unto the Lord; Behold, Lord, the half of my goods I give to the poor; and if I have taken any thing from any man by false accusation, I restore him fourfold.

ST LUKE 19:8

21

22

23

24

25

26

27

OCTOBER

And he that was dead came forth, bound hand and
foot with graveclothes: and his face was bound about
with a napkin. Jesus saith unto them, Loose him, and
let him go.

ST JOHN 11:44

28

29

30

31

1

2

3

OCT – NOV

And they that went before, and they that followed, cried, saying, Hosanna; Blessed is he that cometh in the name of the Lord.

ST MARK 11:9

4

5

6

7

8

9

10

✢ NOVEMBER ✢

And they come to Jerusalem: and Jesus went into the temple, and began to cast out them that sold and bought in the temple, and overthrew the tables of the moneychangers, and the seats of them that sold doves.

ST MARK 11:15

11

12

13

14

15

16

17

NOVEMBER

ST MARK

18

19

20

21

22

23

24

NOVEMBER

Be ye therefore perfect, even as your Father which is in heaven is perfect.
ST MATTHEW 5:48

25
26
27
28
29
30
1

NOV – DEC

But the angel said unto him, Fear not, Zacharias: for
thy prayer is heard; and thy wife Elisabeth shall bear
thee a son, and thou shalt call his name John.
ST LUKE 1:13

2

3

4

5

6

7

8

DECEMBER

And it came to pass, that, when Elisabeth heard the salutation of Mary, the babe leaped in her womb; and Elisabeth was filled with the Holy Ghost.

ST LUKE 1:41

9

10

11

12

13

14

15

DECEMBER

And Joseph also went up from Galilee, out of the city of Nazareth, into Judaea, unto the City of David, which is called Bethlehem; (because he was of the house and lineage of David:)
To be taxed with Mary his espoused wife, being great with child.

ST LUKE 2:4-5

16

17

18

19

20

21

22

✥ DECEMBER ✥

And she brought forth her firstborn son, and wrapped
him in swaddling clothes, and laid him in a manger;
because there was no room for them in the inn.

ST LUKE 2:7

23

24

25

26

27

28

29

DECEMBER

For, behold, from henceforth all generations shall call me blessed.

ST LUKE 1:48

30

31

DECEMBER

And, lo, the angel of the Lord came upon them, and the glory of the
Lord shone round about them: and they were sore afraid.

ST LUKE 2:9

ACKNOWLEDGEMENTS

KEY: (BOD) = Bodleian Library, Oxford   (GIR) = Photographie Giraudon   (SOTH) = By courtesy of Sotheby's   (LOUR) = Studio Lourmel   (SOA) = By courtesy of the Trustees of the Sir John Soane Museum   (BLIB) = British Library   (CIV) = Museo Civico, Turin   (BIB) = Bibliothèque Nationale, Paris
Cover illustration: Pol de Limbourg, Très riches heures de Jean, duc de Berry, MS 65, folio 173r Musée Condé, Chantilly (GIR)
Back cover illustration: The Manderscheid Hours (SOTH)
Illustration opposite title page: Auct D. inf 2.11 f66v (BOD); *opposite title verso:* Master of Charles V, The Arenberg Missal, folio 68v (SOTH)
Picture sources in order of appearance, references are to the manuscript and folio number:
Auct D. inf 2.11 f74v (BOD); 15th century Venetian manuscript Musée Marmottan, Paris/Wildenstein Collection (LOUR); Corpus Christi 410 f22v (BOD); Auct D. inf 2.11 f93v (BOD); The Soane Hours, folio 27v (SOA); Auct D inf 2.11 f39v (BOD); Jean Fouquet, Hours of Etiènne Chevalier, MS 71, folio 31 Musée Condé, Chantilly (GIR); Roll 189N.3 f5 (BOD); Hours of William, Lord Hastings, Add. MS 54782, folio 265v (BLIB); Milan Hours of Jean, duc de Berry, folio 30v (CIV); Auct D inf 2.11 f62v (BOD); Pol de Limbourg, Très riches heures de Jean, duc de Berry, MS 65, folio 143r Musée Condé, Chantilly (GIR); Canon Bibl Lat 62 f25v (BOD); Milan Hours of the duc de Berry, folio 38v (CIV); The Soane Hours, folio 15v (SOA); Hours of Etiènne Chevalier, MS 71, folio 18 Musée Condé, Chantilly (GIR); Jean Fouquet, Hours of Etiènne Chevalier, MS 71, folio 19 Musée Condé, Chantilly (GIR); Auct D inf 2.11 f91v (BOD); Master of Charles V, The Arenberg Missal, folio 68v (SOTH); Pol de Limbourg, Très riches heures de Jean, duc de Berry, MS 65, folio 156v Musée Condé, Chantilly (GIR); Hours of Philippe le Bon, duc de Bourgogne, MS 9511, folio 180r Bibliothèque Royale Albert 1er, Brussels; Corpus Christi 410 f159 (BOD); Corpus Christi 410 f161 (BOD); Pol de Limbourg, Très riches heures de Jean, duc de Berry, MS 65, folio 122v Musée Condé, Chantilly (GIR); Pol de Limbourg, Très riches heures de Jean, duc de Berry, MS 65, folio 184r Musée Condé, Chantilly (GIR); Book of Hours, Harley MS 2897, folio 188 (BLIB); Douce 311 f8v (BOD); Douce 311 f25v (BOD); Auct D inf 2.11 f40v (BOD); Douce 212 f193v (BOD); Corpus Christi 410 f40 (BOD); Très riches heures de Jean, duc de Berry, MS 65, folio 161v Musée Condé, Chantilly (GIR); Petites heures de Jean, duc de Berry, MS Latin 18014, folio 208 (BIB); Workshop of the Master of the Geneva Latini, Book of Hours of the Use of Coutances, Normandy, folio 152 (SOTH); Corpus Christi 410 f47 (BOD); Corpus Christi 410 f49 (BOD); Pol de Limbourg, Très riches heures de Jean, duc de Berry, MS 65, folio 166r Musée Condé, Chantilly (GIR); Corpus Christi 410 f54v (BOD); Corpus Christi 410 f105v (BOD); The Soane Hours, folio 29v (SOA); The Loire Master, Tilliot Hours, Yates Thompson MS 5, folio 70v (BLIB); 15th century French gospel Musée Marmottan, Paris/Wildenstein Collection (LOUR); The Manderscheid Hours (SOTH); Master of Charles V, The Arenberg Missal, folio 13v (SOTH); Corpus Christi 410 f73v (BOD); Douce 212 f181v (BOD); Douce 134 f158v (BOD); Pol de Limbourg, Très riches heures de Jean, duc de Berry, MS 65, folio 43v Musée Condé, Chantilly (GIR); Book of Hours by the Master of James IV of Scotland, Add. MS 35313, folio 76v (BLIB); Bible Moralisée, Naples, MS français 9561, folio 132v (BIB); Auct D. inf 2.11 f66v (BOD); Douce 311 f95v (BOD); Simon Marmion Hours, Salting Collection 1221, folios 85v-86r Victoria & Albert Museum, London